Spiritual Gifts

The Power That Drives You And The Congregation

Neal R. Boese

Fairway Press
Lima, Ohio

SPIRITUAL GIFTS

FIRST EDITION
Copyright © 1995 by
Neal R. Boese

Library of Congress Catalog Card Number: 95-60997

ISBN 0-7880-0615-0
PRINTED IN U.S.A.

This book is dedicated to:

Marsha — my wife, confidant and advocate whose gifts remind me daily of God's continuing love and presence. DiAne, Karen, Brian and Mitch — my children — very special and unique gifts of love.

And to:

St. John Lutheran — Grand Prairie, Texas
Messiah Lutheran — Austin, Texas
House of Prayer Lutheran — San Antonio, Texas
First St. Paul Lutheran — Hastings, Nebraska
Gloria Dei Lutheran — Crestview Hills, Kentucky

Congregations I have served who have brought me to the point that I could write this book.

Table Of Contents

Foreword

I have served as a parish pastor in the Evangelical Lutheran Church in America for eight years and in its predecessor church, the Lutheran Church In America, for 22 years. For the first 15 years of my ministry, the subject of spiritual gifts was not of any particular interest. I was aware of spiritual gifts through the writings of Saint Paul, but neither the seminary I attended nor the denomination I served ever mentioned this subject except in passing. Thus, I honestly had no exposure to spiritual gifts as important ingredients of twentieth century church life.

How tragic this oversight has been for the church! I believe that this lack of understanding concerning spiritual gifts has been a major reason for the apathy affecting many congregations today and the burnout occurring among our church leadership. During the last 30 years, mainline denominations have seen hundreds of parishes close and millions of members leave either to join other denominations or to quit the Church altogether. I believe a lack of focus on spiritual gifts has been a significant contributing factor.

Without question, spiritual gifts are the powers that move the congregation to fulfill its mission. The understanding and usage of these gifts are as necessary for congregational life as oxygen is necessary for human life. When a congregation is empowered with the use of these gifts, it is incredible what happens.

In 1989, I wrote a book called *Why Can't We Grow? We Can!* and, in 1991, another titled *Seven Steps And You Will Grow*. From their titles it is obvious that these books were written about the need for congregations to be involved in evangelism. In each book I presented a chapter on spiritual gifts. I cannot assume that you have read my other books; therefore in the pages that follow I will repeat the theological basis for spiritual gifts as well as relate some of my own experiences with these gifts.

I am most grateful to Gloria Dei Lutheran Church, Crestview Hills, Kentucky, the congregation I am now serving, for giving me the time to write this book and, above all, for making spiritual gifts a significant focus of congregational life.

Finally, a word of thanks: to David and Marta Poling-Goldenne, leaders of evangelism in the Evangelical Lutheran Church in America, for encouraging me to write about this subject; to John Huenniger, a colleague and fellow member of Gloria Dei, for his editing skills; and to my wife Marsha for her constant love and support throughout this project.

It is my hope that through this book spiritual gifts will become real for you and a source of strength for the congregation you serve.

Chapter 1

The Theological Basis

We cannot begin this book simply by listing the spiritual gifts and giving some definitions. We must first understand why they exist and the means our Lord uses to deliver these gifts to His followers. Clearly seen in the theological basis is the fact that these gifts do not just happen to exist nor are they given for any old purpose. The gifts are intentionally given and they are given for a *specific* purpose.

To understand, we must go back to the first book of the Bible and to that famous Garden of Eden. The Garden of Eden was the perfect place, the perfect environment for God's children. Adam and Eve enjoyed the Garden and took responsibility for it. It had everything they could possibly want or need. There was only one problem. There was a specific tree whose fruit was off limits to them. God had forbidden Adam and Eve to eat of the fruit of this tree. But God's condition was too much for Adam and Eve and eventually they ate of the forbidden fruit. This rebellion against God's will, better known as sin, entered and caused a significant problem for Adam and Eve and eventually all of mankind.

With this rebellion, Adam and Eve were banished from the Garden, and a guard was placed in front of the gate to make sure they did not return. But this did not separate God from His children nor would it separate God's intent to reunite His children with His kingdom. The purpose of the Bible is to make known the means He would use for this reunification.

Basic to the plan God designed would be a group of people. A specific group of people were selected to be the conduit for enabling this plan to be carried out. The first group of people selected were the Israelites. God went to Abraham and told him that he would be the father of a great nation and that this nation would be a blessing to all the nations on earth. They would be a blessing by helping all the nations of the world to understand God's plan of salvation. Therefore their task was to share this message with the world. Further, God told them to complete their task; He would give them the necessary tools.

It wasn't long before the nation of Israel became confused as to what it meant to be "chosen." From their perspective, they were chosen solely to receive God's benefits; God was to meet whatever needs they had, which often times meant destroying their enemies. The thought that they existed to serve other nations and to bring to them a plan of salvation was forgotten.

This misunderstanding is made clear in the Old Testament Book of Jonah. Jonah was a follower of God and considered himself very faithful. One day God came to Jonah and told him that he had been chosen to deliver a message to the King of Ninevah. Ninevah had become "sin city" and God was so angry with their sinfulness that in forty days He was going to destroy the city and all its inhabitants. God wanted the King and the people to understand why this would be happening if they didn't change their ways.

Jonah felt that being a messenger was beyond what it meant to be faithful and so he decided to run away. He went down to the sea and got into one of the boats going anywhere but Ninevah. The boat set sail. But before long the winds came up, the waves started rising and the boat and its inhabitants were in trouble. The men on board surmised that the gods must be angry with one of them and, through the casting of lots, determined that Jonah was the one. To save themselves, they tossed him overboard.

In the sea, Jonah was about to drown when all of a sudden a big fish appeared and swallowed him whole. Jonah was washed into the belly of the fish. Here he repented. The fish then vomited and Jonah ended up on land. This time he decides to go to Ninevah to complete the task given to him by God.

He tells the King what the people have done, why God is so angry with them and that God is going to destroy them in forty days. The King hears what Jonah says, recognizes their corporate sinfulness, goes to the people and calls upon them to seek repentance from God. This is precisely what God wants from them. He hears their cry of repentance and forgives them of their sin. Reunification between God and the people of Ninevah now occurs and the Kingdom is open to the people.

One would think the story would end here, but that is not the case. Jonah is now very angry with what has transpired. When God asks him why he is so angry, Jonah says he is angry because God has let the Ninevites off the hook. Because they have repented, God is no longer going to destroy them. Thus, the story ends.

I have gone into detail with the story of Jonah to describe the problem that has presented itself throughout history, the problem of what it means to be chosen by God. In most cases, to be chosen is construed only in terms of the privileges that it will bring. From this perspective God will take care of meeting needs and making the journey through life much easier. Also, it is only to those chosen that God's benefits will be given.

This becomes clear when Jesus enters the world. He talks about all people as God's people. Forgiveness is the primary characteristic of a child of God. The Israelite leadership could not accept this and rejected Him as their Messiah. What He said was too foreign to the leaders' way of thinking.

When Jesus rises from the grave, He brings together the group of people who have been with Him through His ministry and gives them the commission to "go into all the world teaching and baptizing." In other words, a new group of people are now chosen to carry out the commission first given to Abraham: to be a blessing to all the nations of the world.

The disciples and Saint Paul do go and spread the message. Through their Spirit-led efforts many are converted to Christianity. With these conversions, new "groups of people" are ordained to carry out God's plan of salvation. These new "groups of people" are called congregations.

The congregation is now given the task to carry out the commission first given to Abraham and then given to the disciples; to be a blessing to all the people on earth, to teach and baptize and to bring all of God's children into a saving relationship with Him. The job is awesome.

In fact, the job is impossible unless God provides the power to fulfill the task. In the Old Testament, He provided the power directly by constantly intervening when the need developed. When Moses complained that he did not have the skills necessary to lead the Israelites, God provided those skills through his brother Aaron. When the Israelites wanted a king, God gave them a king. Whenever they were hungry, He provided food and so on. In the New Testament, Jesus met the needs of the disciples directly. He provided them with understanding, and He gave them powers to accomplish His purpose.

When He ascended into heaven, the disciples were left to carry out the mission. They were told to go to Jerusalem and preach the Gospel. They were fearful, unsure if they could accomplish the task. Peter was preaching on Pentecost; he was beginning to believe his effort would prove fruitless. He was speaking, but no one was listening. His words were not making any difference to the listeners.

Then the Spirit came, imparting to Peter a gift. He now had the gift of speaking in such a way that people heard, understood and responded. More and more of God's children were getting the message of salvation and as they received that message, they came together into congregations in order to carry that message out into the world.

As they were baptized and came together into congregations, the Spirit provided the power for the congregations to fulfill the mission. And the power provided was spiritual gifts.

When one is baptized, one is given a gift or a mix of gifts that is to be used to enable the mission to be fulfilled. In scripture, baptism never exists just for the person's own welfare; it exists as the calling mechanism God uses to marshal the forces that will be needed to get the job done.

As one baptized, God chooses me to be a part of His saving plan. It is not because I volunteered or am so multi-talented. I do not necessarily yet know why I am chosen, but it has occurred and it is my calling to fulfill that responsibility whatever it may prove to be. He calls me into the Church and, along with the gifts entrusted to others, my gift is used to bring others into God's saving plan.

Finally, I have no doubts that God can use the Church as a whole body to further His mission. I have no doubts that He can use individual denominations to fulfill that mission. And for that work to occur, it takes the spiritual gifts of those who are baptized. But the basic unit of the Church is the congregation. For the purposes of this book, I will focus on the congregation and how the gifts can be used to enable that work to be done.

To summarize the theological basis for spiritual gifts:

1. God's plan of salvation exists to reunite His children with Himself and His kingdom.

2. This plan is carried out through a chosen group of people.

3. The chosen group of people were the Israelites, then the disciples and now the Christian Church.

4. The basic unit that enables the Christian Church to fulfill its mission is the congregation.

5. The power that enables the congregation to fulfill its mission comes through baptism.

6. At baptism, the Holy Spirit enters, a call to service is extended and a spiritual gift is given.

7. This spiritual gift is specific in nature and is to be used to fulfill the mission of God whenever and wherever the opportunity is presented.

Chapter 2

My Personal Experience

I was born in 1939 to Hans and Maidye Boese. My parents were very active in the Lutheran Church and, almost from birth, the congregation was the center of my life. Rarely did we miss Sunday worship or the church school. I was confirmed at the age of 14 after two intensive years of study and was very active in the youth group.

When I graduated from high school, I went to Wittenberg University, a Lutheran school in Springfield, Ohio. There I was active in the religious life of the campus and attended worship most every Sunday. Following college, I entered the seminary located on the same campus.

Seminary life proved to be three of the happiest years of my life. The students were close to one another and to the faculty. Many evenings would be spent in dialogue with the faculty concerning some doctrine or practice of the church. In 1964, I graduated from the seminary and went to my first congregation.

I mention the early days of my life to point out my activity level in the congregation and my exposure to the beliefs and practices of the church. I had no reason to doubt any of the beliefs of the church nor did I think anything was missing in my understanding of congregational life. My background in the church and my studies clearly identified what the church was about and the way faith should be lived out in the congregation.

But something was missing! Spiritual gifts were not identified either in my upbringing or in my religious training as being significant for my life or the life of a congregation. When I accepted "the call" to my first congregation, I had no idea what spiritual gifts were all about nor did I have any understanding as to their application for the congregation.

I must be honest and say that I don't know why spiritual gifts were not a focus of the Lutheran Church. I do remember that whenever the subject would come up it was always in regard to speaking in tongues, and neither I nor my colleagues had any interest in dealing with that issue. We were afraid of it not only because of its emotional nature but also because the experiences some Lutheran congregations had with this subject proved to be negative. In most cases, the congregations had large schisms within their memberships or had closed altogether. So I didn't have any desire to get too close to such matters.

With regard to congregational life, I had come to believe that the power to move the congregation came from the faith of the members, their willingness to participate in the life of the congregation and through the use of their own personal talents. In my view, talents were given at birth and had been developed through the years. Some members were more talented than others with regard to church life and practice but that seemed normal. Some of the members' talents could be used in the congregation more so than others, such as teaching or singing. The talents themselves were not nearly as important as the willingness to serve. Therefore when a particular need would arise in the parish, any warm body would do as long as they were willing. If a position was open on the church council or in our church school, very rarely did the talents of a person come to mind as the chief prerequisite for filling the position. Rather it was the activity level of that person in the congregation or whether they had indicated on a "time and talent sheet" their own particular interest in the area needing a volunteer.

Time and talent sheets were often the basis for determining who would serve in any particular area. Time and talent sheets were forms filled out in the fall each year listing all the areas where one could serve in the congregation. Everything from communion assistant to plumber was listed and the hope was that all members would sign up to serve in some area of congregational life. It was not so much their own talents that were important; it was their commitment to the church. If the member was committed, the member would sign up somewhere and hopefully in areas that were the hardest to fill. I cringe as I write these words, but I want to be honest in explaining the way I viewed congregational life and member participation.

I served two congregations in Texas before moving in 1973 to San Antonio. It was here that I discovered the power and significance of spiritual gifts. But it took an extraordinary experience for this to happen.

In 1975, the congregation had grown to approximately 500 baptized members. That was a large Lutheran congregation in Texas as our denomination was just beginning to impact and most of the congregations were in their infant stages. What concerned the leadership of our congregation was the fact that, throughout the Lutheran Church, 500 baptized members was about as large as congregations would grow. Then, for some unknown reason, the congregations would start decreasing in size. We did not want that to happen. So we decided to study congregations that had continued growing through the years and had no history of declining membership.

Our leadership made contact with three denominations: the Presbyterian Church-USA, the United Methodist Church and the Lutheran Church in America. We wanted the names and locations of those congregations that had grown steadily for 25 years or more. We expected to receive a large number of congregations to choose from, but, as it turned out, we received only 38 names. These churches were scattered all over the country and none were in Texas!

We selected the ten closest congregations and made contact with them. To get an idea of who we were dealing with, four congregations were from rural areas, four congregations were in suburban areas and two congregations were located in the inner city of large metropolitan areas. Since one member of our congregation had an airplane at his disposal, this made it a little bit easier for us to get around so we could study each of the congregations.

17

We began by writing and stating our interest in studying each congregation. All ten congregations were very willing to work with us and we began the study. First, we made contact through a questionnaire, then we went to visit. In visiting the congregations, we expected to find much of what occurred in the life of our congregation. We expected this not because we had such a high opinion of who we were, but simply because we were growing in membership and assumed that others were growing in the same ways.

We expected to find the strength of these congregations in six major areas:

1. strong worship experiences with good music and preaching;

2. good education programs, particularly with regard to children's education;

3. youth programs that impacted both on the youth of the congregation and youth in the community;

4. good service oriented outreach programs into the community;

5. strong, aggressive follow-up on visitors to the worship services;

6. strong lay participation.

As it turned out, all ten parishes did have good, solid programming in the areas mentioned. However, that which had allowed their continued growth to occur was not among those that I have mentioned, and that was quite a jolt.

Before I go any further, I want to mention a fact made very clear to us as we talked with the congregations' leaders. None of these congregations had reached the point where they were without having gone through tremendous upheaval. All of these congregations had been of a traditional nature within their own denomination with most of the ministry carried out by the ordained pastor with lay assistance. Evangelism did not exist except to those who found their way to these churches on their own and accepted what they had to offer.

Then, in every case, a pastor had come who refused to do things the old way and believed fervently in the *ministry* of the laity. Another interesting element was that, in all cases, the congregations had gone outside of denomination sources to find assistance in making the transition from a congregation led by the ordained alone to a congregation led by both ordained and laity — with each having very clear job descriptions. The primary change was with the role of the pastor and the pastor's own desire and belief that all members of the parish were called there to serve in some specific way. That change in thinking was critical.

With that in mind, let's go back and see what was discovered. What we found as essential was, first, a good solid education program. But rather than the focus being with the children, it was a focus on adult learning. All ten congregations had a large number of Bible study groups with fellowship and education being the prime ingredients. We found that in all the educational programs of the congregations, the thrust was on the mission of the church; that is: "What are we about as the church?" "What is the role of each member in fulfilling that mission?" The mission statement of each congregation guided everything it did and studied. The key to their learning experiences was to enable each participant to understand why the church existed in the first place, the role of the congregation, and what each member is called to do in order to fulfill that mission.

In every instance, the purpose of the church was to assist all members to grow in faith and, once mobilized, to reach out with the saving message of Jesus Christ to those outside of the church. That mission was clear and every member understood this to be the purpose. It was also clear that members who did not accept the congregation's mission statement were helped either to come to this understanding or to find another church home. This was not done in a harsh way; it was done with the belief that what their mission statement said was, indeed, their role and if everyone was not in agreement, the work of the congregation would never be done.

The second essential within these congregations was a focus on spiritual gifts. When we discovered this fact, we almost

19

quit the study. Personally, I did not want to continue since I did not understand this to be a major element within the Lutheran Church. I had my own biases as to what it meant to be involved in spiritual gifts. By the grace of God, however, we did continue the study, but it took a particularly incredible experience for the impact of spiritual gifts to strike home.

From our study of these congregations, we had recognized a shared ministry that existed between the laity and the ordained. Lay members participated in areas of church life, which, from our experience, had always been relegated only to the ordained. For instance, during the worship service, lay members assisted in leading the liturgy, sermons were given by lay members and the laity assisted with Holy Communion. While that is very common in almost all mainline denominations today, that was not the case in the 1970s.

So we started sharing the ministry of our congregation in the same ways and this was received very well. At first, the longtime Lutherans had a problem with this new approach, but, before long, no one thought too much about it. In fact, it became one of those areas of our congregation's life that drew many new people.

I decided that if we were really going to share the ministry, then we needed involvement in other areas of congregational life, too, especially in areas normally seen as applying only to the ordained. One evening I went to the church council with a proposal. There were twelve members of the council and each member was assigned one month of the year. During his or her assigned month, the council member would go with me if I received any kind of emergency call at night. The assigned member would not be called on if the emergency was a counseling situation; but if there was a death or someone was rushed to the hospital, the council member would go with me. The council agreed to participate.

At first, the few emergencies which did occur were not all that frightening. But one night it changed. I received a call about 4 a.m. from a member of the congregation. It seemed that one of his relatives had shot and killed his wife and oldest son, then turned the gun on himself. There were three other children who were there throughout the tragedy, but, for some unexplained reason, had not been hurt. I was asked to come and see if I could be of any help. This was not exactly what one would call a normal emergency, but what came out of this experience changed my view of congregational life and practice. It also changed John's life.

John was the council member on call that month. When I called him, I did not tell him the circumstances as I doubted if he would have gone with me. Rather, I drove by to pick him up and on the way to see the children I laid out the situation. As we were driving along, John became very silent and perspiration began to appear on his forehead. I could see this from the lights on the street. Finally, after I explained the whole situation, John informed me that under no circumstances was he going to enter that house. He gave a number of reasons such as he would get sick at the sight of blood. He had never been around a dead body and would probably pass out. But above all, he had no training whatsoever in this kind of situation. So what help could he be? By the time he had finished with all the reasons why he did not want to go into the house, we had arrived. Reluctantly, he agreed to go in with me.

The situation was about as bad as you could imagine. Blood was all over the place. Fortunately, the bodies had been taken away so we didn't have to be a part of that scene. But when we arrived, we found the three children huddled off to the side of a back room, clinging to one another and not uttering a sound. They seemed to be almost catatonic. People were starting to arrive, and I was summoned to the front room; John stayed behind with the children.

Throughout the time we were there, I saw John working with these children in a way that amazed me. He seemed to know exactly what to do. After a while he had them crying, then talking and starting to react as one would expect in a situation such as this. The skills he used were of tremendous help to these children.

21

At the next council meeting, we were talking about this situation, and I mentioned how helpful John had been. I looked at him and asked if they were skills he had learned someplace. How did he know what to do? He looked at me with this perplexed expression wondering what I was talking about. He had no idea that what he had done was so exceptional. He assumed that it was the same thing anyone would do under such circumstances. We reached a point in our discussion when all of us sitting around the table went silent. And the same thought hit all of us. What are we dealing with here? What kind of power do we see operating? Maybe there *is* something to be said for spiritual gifts. We had heard others talking about the power that is generated through these gifts, but to be honest we did not take these comments too seriously, that is, until now.

As John began to realize he had a gift and as we started studying more about these gifts, John found that his gift was a gift of mercy: the gift of being able to feel the need that someone has and then doing something to meet that need.

With the recognition of this gift, the place John was serving in the congregation changed. John was an auto mechanic, and he was serving on the property committee. We thought that this committee was the place he could best use his talent of repairing or fixing things around the church buildings. Never did he have any notion that God had called him into the congregation for another reason.

Once he discovered this gift, he began to use it in ways he would never have envisioned. Near the congregation was a very large hospital complex. It was the mid-1970s, and the work of Dr. Elizabeth Kubler-Ross was affecting many people. Her studies with those in terminal illness indicated that most caregivers, including nurses, doctors, ministers, as well as family members, were staying away from the dying because they just did not know what to do. John led a core of members who would visit in the hospital. They would visit those people dying. Can you imagine the impact they made? That was the reason John was called to this congregation: to impact on the lives of people who were being forgotten.

That experience changed my view of spiritual gifts and began a process that led me into a whole new approach to congregational life. It helped me understand the power of God that was laying dormant simply because it was not being utilized.

Congregations are storehouses of power waiting to be mobilized and unleashed. What a difference it would make in congregations if they truly believed in gifts and worked to understand and use them. I have seen one congregation after another that does not believe it has anything to offer or there is nothing more it can do other than what is being done. There is apathy and conflict as the congregation struggles to exist. Yet within that same congregation is this powerful resource that will not only cause it to truly come alive but also to fulfill God's mission in that place.

Since the mid-1970s, I have seen lives change as people become aware of spiritual gifts. Individuals on the periphery of congregational life or getting burned out are being reborn as a whole new world opens up and God uses them in ways never foreseen.

Dave always had a feeling that music was to be a part of his life; but in his mind, he couldn't play an instrument very well, couldn't sing very well, nor was he able to read a note of music. This told him that his feeling was just that, a feeling, and was not real. One Sunday morning he heard a sermon concerning spiritual gifts, a sermon given as we were introducing gifts into the congregation. For a reason he now understands, he saw this sermon as directly aimed at him to proceed with his feeling for music. He took his guitar out of the closet where it had lain for years, dusted it off and started working with it.

Today Dave provides instrumental and vocal music for many of our services, particularly the outdoor services we have each summer. He has recorded his music, written songs and plays in many locations believing with all his heart that God wants his music to be a means of moving others toward Him. His music is bluegrass gospel music, the kind of music not often heard in Lutheran congregations; and yet in this suburban, sophisticated area, his music and his witness have been a source of real inspiration.

Dave has told his story in the congregation and to others and has been extraordinarily helpful in leading others to discover their gifts. If you would talk with Dave about his experience, he would just shake his head and say he has no idea how all this came about nor any idea of the opportunities it would open up. He can only thank God for this new life of music and service.

Two stories may not seem like much in the way of evidence. But these are just two examples out of many that I have witnessed. My own personal experience began with skepticism and concluded with a certainty that with the power of spiritual gifts at work, no congregation can help but fulfill its mission and change lives. This road began twenty years ago. There is still a long way to go, but it is exciting and, as I lay out before you my view of the gifts, their definitions and how they can be used in the congregation, I hope it will be helpful as you journey down the same road. We will look at one gift at a time, and I will introduce you to some people who possess the gift identified and tell you their stories. In chapter six, I will present an inventory that will help you determine what your gift might be.

Chapter 3

The Gifts

1. Administration

The gift of administration is the gift that enables a believer to formulate, direct and carry out plans necessary to fulfill a purpose.

I have conducted spiritual gift workshops for several years and rarely have I conducted one in which the gift of administration was not challenged. Even though Saint Paul lists it as one of the gifts in 1 Corinthians 12:28 and even though its usage is vital to the work of the congregation, for some reason many cannot see this gift as having anything to do with that which is spiritual. Therefore it is good that we start with this gift for it makes clear that in order for the congregation to function there is much that is needed, and the gifts that are needed are not always the ones we think of in the congregation.

Administration has gained a negative reputation because it means many things to many people. For many pastors, when the word administration is mentioned, it has to do with typing the Sunday bulletin, putting it through the copier, folding and placing the finished product on the usher stand. It involves busy work, the details that are weekly carried out in the church office. But the fact is administration has little if anything to do with this concept, and the gift of administration is vital to the welfare of the congregation.

Since this is a gift that I have been blessed with, the explanation will come from my own perspective. The gift is a gift of perception and implementation. When I am given a goal that someone or some group has in mind, my immediate thought is not the end result but the means to achieve the results.

For instance, a building program is proposed. The needs are clear and the amount and usage of space that will be capable of meeting those needs are determined. My first thought is the plan that must be put into effect in order to reach the desired goal. I think of the size of a task force that will be needed to implement the plan, the kind of expertise that will be needed on the task force, the order in which the plan must be carried out and the time line that will be needed to get the job done.

Once the plan is clearly in mind, I proceed to delegate, motivate and organize. I see this as a normal way of getting things done and the only logical way to do it. I mention the words normal and logical because for years I did not consider my ability to perceive and carry out a plan as a gift. I assumed everyone could do it; some just did it better than others. How wrong I was.

Without doubt, people can learn to be administrators. The number of workshops and seminars on this subject is high. To have the gift does not mean that one does not have to grow in understanding or expand on the knowledge of the subject. What it means is that in carrying out the responsibilities involved there is great joy and satisfaction. I thrive on opportunities this gift allows, and I find it easy to get done what needs to be done. Certainly there are frustrations involved when dealing with people and unknowns, but overall I am the happiest when involved in this kind of responsibility.

I am driven by this gift to use it in the life of the congregation. A person with this gift should be called upon when a plan is needed to reach an established goal or when someone is needed to direct a program that could involve a number of steps to complete.

Not long ago, the education division of the congregation was looking for a director for our church school. The church school is large with a well developed program. The education division had been searching for weeks to find a new director. Requests had gone out for a volunteer and many telephone calls had been made to possible candidates. When the need was made known during the church board meeting, I suggested that the spiritual gift inventories should be checked to see if there would be any who possessed the gifts that would meet this need. In discussing the gifts that would be needed, it was suggested that the gift of teaching was the vital gift, as the person chosen would be working with teachers and would be working within a teaching situation. Yet the fact was teaching skills weren't needed; administrative skills were. We looked under the gift of administration, found a member who had that gift, made one telephone call and the person not only accepted, but was very grateful that she had been asked. It was not a person we would have thought of without the spiritual gift emphasis and understanding.

I can just hear you now saying, "Yeah, right! That doesn't always work." You're right. But more often than not it does work when we consider people and positions from an entirely different perspective. In this case, an administrator was needed and one was found.

As mentioned, this doesn't always happen. But it is better than the old system of finding any warm body or someone just willing to volunteer. One with the gift of administration does not have to necessarily be knowledgeable in the area of need. Rather, the need is to have someone who can visualize and implement a plan to achieve the goal.

To have the gift of administration allows the believer to serve the congregation in any position whereby planning and the carrying out of a plan is needed. Those with the gift serve well on the church board, leading groups, organizations and task forces. But one note of caution. The gift is not used well when it involves the doing of a plan, the carrying out of all the details. One with the gift is the dreamer, the developer, the motivator and the implementor. Put in the right place, one with this gift will greatly aid the congregation is getting a task done in an orderly and complete way and do so with enthusiasm.

2. Apostle

Apostle is the gift that gives a believer the courage and the urgency to express faith in settings where the Gospel is rarely heard.

Whenever I think of apostle, immediately there come to my mind the great Biblical leaders. Saints Peter, Paul, Matthew, James and John are just a few. I think of those who carried the faith into pagan lands, were persecuted for what they preached, yet brought the Christian faith to a point where eventually the entire Roman Empire would become Christian. We are talking about the giants of faith and those who, in most instances, were executed because of their perseverance of belief. They were extraordinary individuals.

Therefore when the gift of apostle is considered, thoughts immediately turn toward those who would serve in hostile environments and die for their faith. One would think of missionaries in foreign lands, followers of Christ who for years worked underground in Communist lands. We think of the Dietrich Bonhoeffers of the world, those who spoke out in faith when it was far from the popular thing to do and did not back down when threatened with death. These are indeed the ones possessing the gift of apostle. So what is the gift and how can we relate this to our own congregational settings and to individual believers with whom we work and live every day?

Saint Paul obviously had the gift of apostle. What characteristics of this gift can we learn from him? We think of his standing before hostile people and the courage that had to be present. We think of the numerous attempts to silence him and the zealousness and tenacity with which he continued his work. We think of the many times he went into environments that were far from pleasant to speak the Word and say things very few present wanted to hear. We think of the lack of patience he had for those of faith who would show signs of backing off and not being counted when faith was on the line. We think of his "no nonsense" attitude with regard to congregations

28

that he had started or were requesting his help. All in all, we think of a very brave person who could not be stopped from presenting the faith.

The gift of apostle does include courage, tenacity, perseverance and zealousness, but that is not the gift. The gift itself is a gift of love, a profound love that motivates all actions. The gift enables the believer to understand clearly how much love Jesus Christ has for His children and how far our Lord will go to save His children. The gift bearer feels this love and recognizes the hopelessness of life without Jesus. The bearer cannot wait to express this love to those who do not understand it.

Therefore the gift results in both inward and outward actions. Inwardly, there is the certainty of God's love and the recognition of all He is doing in this world and among His people. The gift bearer can look into the most hostile of environments and see the love of Jesus. The gift bearer can look into the eyes of the most hostile of people and see that person as a child of God. In the mind of the gift bearer, this is not being courageous. He or she is simply seeing what others cannot see, seeing Christ in action and reflecting that action.

This is the place where the outward action comes in. Having seen Jesus at work and having seen the love He has for His children, the gift bearer takes what is seen and shares with those who cannot see. The love Jesus has for the gift bearer is now reflected in the love the gift bearer has for others. This love causes the gift bearer to go into places not normally reserved for religious thinking in order to share the love of Christ. Where else would one go to share this kind of message than to the place where the love of Jesus is not carried out or known?

Therefore in our contemporary settings, one does not need to go to foreign lands in order to find the nonbeliever. One doesn't need to go far to find all kinds of hostile settings and people hostile to the Word.

Several years ago, a young girl came into my office to share an experience. In her school, the group she ran with was experimenting with drugs. She did not want to get involved. She knew her faith would not allow her to get involved, but the pressure she was under was tremendous. Finally, she was told that either she take one of the substances or she would no longer be a part of this group. Not only did she refuse to take the drug, but she said that something made her stand up and proclaim her faith. She was thrown out of the group and ridiculed to those who did not know all the facts. She lost many of her friends and felt very lonely for a long period of time.

"It was a hard time, but somehow I knew that I wasn't alone. I still cannot believe that I stood up and said what I did, but I looked at all those who had been my friends and I felt sorry for them. Even though they treated me awfully, I still felt sorry for them and wanted to help them. Isn't that crazy?"

It's not crazy at all — especially for someone possessing the gift of apostle. They can see what others cannot see.

Whether it is on the job, in a neighborhood group, in school or among our friends, the opportunities to take a stand with regard to the One in whom we believe are endless. And just as in the past, the responses are often far from pleasant and the repercussions can be harsh. Therefore the gift of apostle becomes a very significant gift, giving the power to be able to withstand all that occurs.

A believer with the gift of apostle can be a powerful witness in the congregation. The person can be utilized for temple talks, sermons and testimonies before groups. But it must be recognized that whenever one with the gift of apostle speaks, those who hear may not always like what they are hearing. Generally the words are confrontational and without tact.

Therefore one note of caution. If one possesses the gift, the evangelism committee might not be the place to serve. This is often times the first thought and may be the place one with this gift would want to serve, but there could be a problem.

I was serving a congregation in Texas and there was a member in the congregation who was always in the church office on Monday morning wanting to know who had visited on Sunday so he could make an evangelism call. Since it was rare that anyone wanted to visit, I had no hesitation in giving him the names. But it also became clear that most of those visited never came back to the congregation. I did not recognize what might have been the problem; I just assumed he simply was not giving them a good impression. However, after learning more about spiritual gifts, I suspect now that he had the gift of apostle for there is a strong tendency to be forceful. And for those who come to worship services as visitors, this kind of approach may steer them away from rather than to the congregation.

We have seen two examples where the gift of apostle has been used in a very positive way and in a not so positive way. The role of the congregation is to assist in channeling the gifts into arenas where the gifts can best be used. When this occurs, lives are changed.

3. Craftsmanship/Artistry

Craftsmanship/Artistry is the gift that gives the believer the skill of creating artistic expressions that produce a spiritual response of strength and inspiration.

Craftsmanship/Artistry is a gift I have seen from early childhood. My father had this gift. He came from Dresden, Germany, in 1912, with his parents, brother and sister. He grew up in Texas; and from as far back as he could remember, he had a desire to become a Lutheran pastor. Unfortunately, his economic circumstances did not allow him to pursue this dream. But early on, he found that drawing pictures came very easily, he felt relaxed and satisfied when he was drawing and, through his drawing, he entered his own means of ministry.

He utilized his gift in the congregations where he belonged. At First Lutheran Church in Nashville, Tennessee, you can see the result of his work: a 40-foot mural in the front of the church depicting the Ascension of our Lord. It has been a source of inspiration for thousands of believers through the years.

In briefly describing a little of my father's circumstances, there are some key words that tell us some things about the gift. "Early," "easy," and "drawn" are three of these key words. "Early" on the gift becomes evident to the receiver. The gift bearer finds it "easy" to be able to do such things as draw or build. Finally, the word "drawn" speaks of the direction one with the gift channels its use. This is the place the gift bearer wants to use this gift and inevitably it is a source of inspiration for many.

Now what is the gift? We see the results, but what is the gift itself? My dad would tell me how he could see in his mind the picture that he was going to draw. He could visualize the way in which it would be produced on canvas and the colors that would be needed. He could see it in his mind and translate that vision onto canvas. It is a hand-eye coordination, the gift of being able to see what you can then bring into reality.

Bill has this gift and it's a source of inspiration to everyone in the congregation I presently serve. Not long ago, we came up with the idea of having name tags for members to wear on Sunday morning. We didn't want to just put the tags on a table where they would lie all week. So we asked Bill to design a container for these tags. Those of us who made the request had in mind some sort of box with openings for each of our families. What Bill built was far from a box. It is a piece of furniture in the church that is a source of inspiration for people as they enter the door. You have to see it to believe what I am saying. In the center of it is the cross and the way it is built makes it very easy to use. I was stunned when I saw it.

However, I shouldn't have been stunned, for Bill has possessed and used this gift for years and his work is deeply appreciated in the congregation. In talking with Bill about his gift, he says the same things as did my father. He can see it in his mind. When a request is made, immediately his mind becomes active with ideas. He sketches out numerous plans, working on them until the right one appears. Then he takes what has been in mind and brings it to life.

When I began writing about spiritual gifts, I separated craftsmanship and artistry. I separated them because of the end result. In the case of craftsmanship the end result was seen in wood, sculpture or pottery — in other words, some solid product. In the case of artistry, the end result would be seen on canvas. Now I have concluded that even though the end products may be different, the gift is the same. It's the gift of being able to see a picture in one's mind and then translate it into a form such as glass or wood, paper or metal that provides inspiration to those who see it.

A congregation is blessed when a believer with this gift is a member. It is a gift that can produce inspiration that will not only affect members of that particular congregation, but it can become a great evangelism tool as well. Those not of the faith have been known to view some particular object or painting and become so moved by it that the beginning of a faith journey for them takes place. The gift is precious and should be utilized.

All too often, I have seen individuals with this gift not being utilized in a congregation. In some instances, they are asked to be "fix it" people. In other words, they repair or fix that which in the church has been broken. Or it is assumed that someone with the gift is too busy to do work in the church and is not asked. The fact is that one with the gift cannot use it enough and what a blessing it would be for the congregation. Paintings that depict events in the life of our Lord, chancel furniture such as an altar, baptismal fonts, pulpit or lectern, banners used in worship processions or to hang on walls throughout the facility, a sign that displays your congregation's name are all examples of ways this gift can be used. The gift bearer has the imagination and skill to produce all sorts of inspiration pieces; all that is needed is the opportunity.

4. Discernment

Discernment is the gift that motivates a believer to seek God's will and purpose and apply that understanding to individual and congregation situations.

Well before I began to recognize the power of spiritual gifts, I knew that Jill had a very special gift that proved very important in the first congregation that I served. Whenever any kind of Bible study would be held, Jill would be there with her Bible, her William Barclay commentaries and her questions. Sometimes her questions would really bother me because she wouldn't just accept some answer; she always wanted more than what I was able to give her. She would probe deeply into Biblical passages that I thought were self-explanatory and, more often than not, would come up with some insight that I had never seen.

Jill's persistence in scriptural study was so evident and so thorough that she became the resource many of us, including me, would go to for insights. Once I got over the threat of having someone in the congregation knowing more than I did about the scriptures, the more exciting it became to hear her understanding of a particular passage. She had this ability to cut through all the words and get to the point.

Her knowledge was such that many in the congregation would go to her in order to understand what God's will might be for them in their own personal circumstances. I would go to her to get ideas as to whether or not she thought the congregation should move in this or that direction. She had a very warm but firm manner and sometimes would say things we didn't want to hear, but we always left believing that what she said was true and was God's will.

Without question Jill had the gift of discernment. When I would talk with her about her intense interest in the scriptures, she seemed surprised that I thought it was unusual. She felt any Christian would have that same interest. She believed there was so much to learn and was so excited with the opportunities for learning, that a day wouldn't go by when she wasn't working on some passage of the Bible. Indeed she was a gift to the congregation.

In thinking about the gift of discernment, it is a gift that moves a person to want to know God's will and to want to know it so badly that the time it takes to acquire this understanding is insignificant. I can remember when she was working on the book of Job. She must have stuck at it for over a year. She searched through commentaries and different Bible translations. And she believed that no matter how much she knew, there was always more to know.

With the understanding the gift brings, there is the motivation to apply this understanding to life situations. The gift bearer is able to see if an action is motivated by an evil force or is in accord with the understanding of Scripture. The gift bearer is not a troublemaker, is not one who just has to point out everything that is wrong within a person or congregation; yet he or she is not hesitant to express this understanding and how it can be applied.

A believer who possesses this gift can be a valuable addition to any teaching staff, but the primary target should be adults. The depth of understanding and the directness of approach may be too much for young people and even for new Christians; but those mature in the faith can profit greatly from this gift bearer.

A believer with this gift can assist the congregation in decision making for not all congregational actions are motivated by the Spirit. The bearer of this gift will help the congregation to stay on track if listened to and understood.

5. Evangelism

Evangelism is the gift that moves believers to reach non-believers in such a way that they are baptized and become active forces in the Christian community.

The gift of evangelism and the gift of apostle have much in common. They are both geared towards reaching those who are not baptized and do not know that Jesus Christ is their Lord and Saviour. Both gifts give to the gift bearers the ability to talk about their faith and the persistence to continue even though their audience may not be receptive.

But the gift of evangelism and the gift of apostle are not the same gift. They are different gifts and both are needed in order to bring someone to the point of baptism and new life in the Church. As mentioned in my description of the gift of apostle, the one with the gift is moved to confront and to express dimensions of faith with those who do not necessarily want to hear what the gift bearer has to say. The direct result may be very negative, but, in the long run, what has been said may lead someone to a relationship with Jesus Christ. That is the point: to express the faith. Whether or not a person responds personally to the gift bearer in a positive way is unimportant.

But that is not the case with regard to the gift of evangelism. Relationships are most important and are needed in order to help people sort through where they have been in their life journeys and how faith in Jesus Christ may lead them in a totally new direction. One Bible example stands out as illustrative of what I mean.

Paul was on his way to Damascus in order to kill Christians. This is what he thought God wanted him to do. But in his confrontation with God along the Damascus road, he not only found this wasn't what God wanted, but also that, instead of serving God, he was serving Satan. He was confused and deeply anguished. Barnabas then entered the picture and became the one to help lead Paul through this time of turmoil. He was the one who helped Paul sort through his priorities. When Paul was converted, Barnabas was the one who stood by him when the disciples wanted to get rid of him. Barnabas was an evangelist for Paul.

In this situation we see what the gift of evangelism brings to a believer. The evangelist is one who so loves another that he will listen and compassionately respond. He will stay with the person when others want to abandon him or go on to try and reach someone else. He does not give up on a nonbeliever even when the nonbeliever is not responding to his words. His persistence, patience and love is that which breaks through and helps a person to make the changes necessary to start a new life with Christ.

Nancy's gift was the gift of evangelism. She was one who would never give up on anyone. She was a lay visitor who made hundreds of calls. And the ones she loved to visit the most were the ones who would not immediately respond to her first visit. In many cases they would tell her they had visited the congregation but did not plan to return. Or they had come because of a baptism, marriage, or funeral of a friend, but had no interest in coming back as they had no particular interest in any church. This was like an open invitation to Nancy. From that point on, her kindness and her persistency and her love for those people was such that eventually many found their way into the congregation. I have never been in a parish that grew as quickly as did this parish and, without any doubt, it was Nancy's gift given to that congregation which caused the growth. Nor have I served a parish made up primarily of people who at one point had no intention of ever making their way into a congregation. Nancy led them through the power of this gift and both those led and the congregation were blessed.

The gift of evangelism is that which leads a person to focus on relationships. Through these relationships, one is led to know and love Jesus Christ. The gift bearer exemplifies the love of Jesus through kindness and persistency. Gift bearers never give up, just as they know our Lord never gives up.

In the congregation, the bearer of this gift is needed on the evangelism committee and in a visitation role. When I have recognized this gift in a believer, I have tried to put this person in a position whereby he or she could be in contact with as many visitors as possible. If, on a church staff, there is a position for lay visitor, this is the gifted person for that task. They thrive on this responsibility and those who are contacted are blessed.

6. Exhortation

Exhortation is a gift that moves the believer to reach out with Christian love and presence to people in personal conflict or facing a spiritual void.

At first glance, the thought would be that one who has the gift of exhortation would be one who is a preacher, who stands before a group of people urging the people to follow Christ or scolding them for not being true to their faith. I think of Billy Sunday or Billy Graham, who in their rallies were known to exhort, to rally people around the conviction that Jesus is their Lord and Saviour. And certainly the word exhortation, from Webster's point of view, would carry this meaning.

But biblically speaking, this is not what the gift of exhortation is about. Hebrews 3:13 describes the gift very well: "But exhort one another every day, as long as it is called 'today,' that none of you may be hardened by the deceitfulness of sin."

Even though our Scriptures make clear that life here on earth is difficult and not without peril, the times in life when we have the most severe crisis of faith are those times when personal difficulty overwhelms us. In my confirmation class for seventh and eighth grade young people, I have a four-week section in which class members can ask any question they would like to ask Jesus if they could meet Him face to face. This opens the door for the confirmands to think through faith issues, especially those giving them some problems. One young student who recently had suffered a loss in the family asked the question, "What did I do so wrong that you would take someone from me?" It is the same question Job asked in the Old Testament and the kind of questions that were asked in the Book of Ecclesiastes. It is the question most of us ask when we are confronted with a personal crisis. We ask these questions because deep within is the belief that if we are faithful, then our Lord and Saviour will make sure that bad things do not happen to us. Therefore when bad things do happen, it violates our belief system and we have a crisis of faith.

With this as a common occurrence for most Christians at some point in their faith journeys, it is essential that one with the gift of exhortation assist when the crisis occurs. One with the gift of exhortation is a counselor, feeling keenly the distress yet understanding that our Lord never promises to remove all distress in life. Rather His promise is to walk through these times with us.

Joan has this gift. Her compassionate nature and her understanding of human conditions compels her to reach out in love to those who are suffering. She has the capacity to hear, accept, advise and respond to those who are suffering. Those who are questioning their faith feel comfortable in relating this to her and, through her counsel and guidance, their faith is often renewed and strengthened.

Most of us find that as we look back on those times when we were in personal crisis, we can see the hand of God working, even though that hand was hidden to us during the crisis. The believer with the gift of exhortation can see the workings of God at the time the crisis is occurring and, through this gift, can relate God's presence in such a way that faith is renewed.

The gift of exhortation is vital to the welfare of a congregation because it is vital to the welfare of individual Christians. As faith is renewed and strengthened within individuals during their times of crisis, this adds significantly to the overall strength of the congregation.

One with the gift of exhortation serves well in the social ministry area of congregation life and is moved toward such programs as a crisis visitation team within the congregation. One with this gift can be a very good teacher among young people and adults. The gift bearer's compassionate nature and ability to articulate spiritual understandings describes well the gift and its usage.

7. Faith

Faith is the gift that gives a believer the eyes to see the Spirit at work and the ability to trust the Spirit's leading with no sense where it all might lead.

The Bible makes it clear that no one can come to faith through his or her own devices. You cannot work hard enough or learn enough to gain faith. You cannot decide for yourself that you want to have faith and then go out and get it. It is a gift that comes through the actions of the Holy Spirit and is given to all believers. Therefore, with this as a theological position, what is unique about the spiritual gift of faith?

Let me tell you about Sylvia, who has the spiritual gift of faith. Her life has been extremely difficult, particularly in the last ten years. She lost her husband to cancer, her two children both died in a boating accident and, because of all the medical bills, her financial situation has been a real source of anxiety. Yet through all of it, her faith has enabled her to manage and be a source of inspiration for the congregation.

In similar circumstances, most Christians find themselves with a crisis of faith. So many hurtful things are happening that to see God's presence is very difficult, but not so with Sylvia. Her faith was always the bulwark that kept her going. Her strength of faith was such that people often asked her how she could continue in that belief. She was always surprised that anyone would ever wonder.

For Sylvia the gift of faith was a certainty, a certainty that in the midst of all that was happening, her Lord was there and was acting in love. She could see countless acts of love and recognized them as coming from God. It was her gift to be able to see and comprehend what others could not see and comprehend.

David also had this gift, although at the time I did not recognize it as a spiritual gift. It was early in my ordained ministry when I met David. He was about ready to retire and, like so many others, had great plans for his retirement years. He and his wife were going to travel all over the world, something they had dreamed about for years but never had the time to do. Then, as so often happens, poor health entered the picture. David had a stroke and, during the time I knew him, he was mostly confined to bed. But every time I would visit him, he would always have a smile and tell me about the blessings that were occurring in his life.

One day David was taken to the hospital. It would be his last stay. He was in very poor condition when I entered the room. There were several machines enabling him to stay alive. Yet when I came near the bed, his face radiated with a smile and a word of cheer. I made some statement about his positive attitude in the midst of all that was happening, and his response opened my eyes to the characteristics of this gift.

"How can I help but feel positive with all the blessings that are happening?" As I was standing there, a nurse came in to tell him that she was going home, but would see him the next day. As she left, she reached down and pinched his toe in a very affectionate sort of way. She left and he looked at me and said, "See, another blessing. God is so good to me."

The uniqueness of this gift is the ability to see God at work and the certainty that, in the midst of all that is happening, good will prevail. This certainty cannot be shaken and it cannot be shaken because, through the eyes of faith, numerous examples of His presence can be seen.

Sylvia and David's faith became examples of faith for their respective congregations. In each case, they became mentors for others going through difficult periods. Particularly was this the case with Sylvia when I came to recognize the gift that she possessed. I would ask her to visit with individuals going through difficult times and she became for them a tremendous source of strength. She could point out blessings that were occurring in their lives, and even though they did not know where their source of strength would lead them, with her counsel they entered the future with confidence.

Ones with this gift can be used as mentors for others. They can be used in temple talks to give inspiration to the congregation. There are many ways in which this gift can be used as it is recognized and put into practice. Primarily it gives those of faith an added measure of faith that can be very helpful both for those individuals and the congregation.

The examples I have given have been ones in which the person with the gift was in some dire circumstance, and this gift was evidenced very clearly. Certainly the gift can be recognized in others not involved in such circumstances, but is simply recognized more clearly in the ways described. Those with the gift of faith recognize clearly the presence of God in all that happens. They are ones with confidence in the future despite the uncertainty of the future.

I have seen in congregational actions those with this gift speaking with optimism of what can occur in the congregation. They are the voices of hope when a congregation finds itself making difficult decisions or involved in difficult situations. I have come to believe that it's in those hard moments of life, both for individuals and congregations, that this gift becomes most evident. And when the voices of those with this gift are heard, individuals and the congregations move forward into the future with renewed strength and vigor. Above all, they move forward with the knowledge and belief that indeed they are being led by the Spirit.

8. Giving

The gift of giving enables a believer to recognize God's blessings and to respond to those blessings by generously and sacrificially giving of one's material resources.

Paul had been through a divorce and was attempting to raise two children without a partner. Financially, he was having a very difficult time, barely able to make ends meet. Whenever commitment time would come in the congregation, he would always pledge an amount that made me want to go to him and say that he ought to cut back, at least for the present, and then increase his pledge when financially he was in a better position. But I would hesitate in doing this because he was so happy to be able to pledge and give.

One afternoon, he came into my office and told me that he had just been given a bonus for the work he had been doing. I was excited for him as this might alleviate some of his financial problems. But then he shocked me by handing me a check equal to half of his bonus. He wanted me to use it for a particular cause being promoted in the congregation. I responded by saying how grateful I was for the check, but couldn't he use this money to alleviate some of his own financial responsibilities? It was then I learned the characteristics of this gift.

He was surprised with my response. He understood where I was coming from, but his surprise was that I didn't understand where he was coming from. He had received this bonus and immediately thought of this project occurring in the church. He saw this bonus as a way of not only helping with his own circumstances, but as a means of helping with this project. God was giving him the money as a blessing, a blessing to be used not only for his needs but for the needs of the church. As I came to see the joy of his gift and his understanding of the material resources that we have, I accepted the gift not only with gratitude but with a renewed appreciation for the spiritual gift of giving.

The gift of giving assists a believer in understanding material resources. Often we think of material resources as coming from our own endeavors. We work for it and deserve what we receive. The gift bearer sees material resources as a gift from God to be used to take care of our own responsibilities, but also to enable the work of the congregation to be enhanced. In addition, the gift gives a believer the recognition of God's presence in life, and it's a means of response. The response is one of joy, and it's one of gratitude in recognition of God's blessings.

When this gift is discussed in workshops, inevitably the question is raised, "Does this apply only to material resources? What about the gift of time and talent?" Certainly a person's usage of time and talent in a joyful way reflects some of these same characteristics. However as I study the Scriptures I find this gift primarily involved with material resources. Jesus makes it a major focus of His teachings, and He does this because our material resources are often the most important focus of our lives. As has often been said, you can look at your checkbook and see where your priorities are.

Therefore God gives to some the gift of giving. The gift bearer radiates a joy that is contagious and also witnesses to the priority of faith in his or her life. This gift bearer can be used as a presenter in visiting specific members during stewardship time to infect the congregation with the joy of giving. Such a gift bearer is a powerful influence on a congregation and upon individual believers.

9. Hospitality

Hospitality is the gift that causes a believer to joyfully open his or her home for meetings and overnight visitors.

In New Testament times, the gift of hospitality was crucial to the development of the Church. When the Church was being started, believers met, often in secret, in people's homes. Since the Roman Empire did not allow religions to be established, the willingness to open up one's home required a significant amount of courage.

Saint Paul mentions several times in his epistles the hospitality shown to him when he came to establish a new congregation. When he would come into a community, he had very little purchasing power so for him to stay for any period of time demanded the giving of food and housing. Since what he said was not always popular, those who provided housing could be under the same attack as he would be. Therefore the gift of hospitality was not only the willingness to use one's home for the purposes of the Church, but also to risk the host's very life.

We live in a very different time. Whenever a pastor/priest comes into a community to speak or preach or organize, housing is provided by the ones inviting. Expenses are paid. There is no threat from outside sources; in other words, it is not against the law to serve a congregation. With this being the present day circumstance, how could the gift even apply to us today?

It applies because of a need that has become most apparent in our present day. We live in a mobile society and, with so much movement, people feel isolated from each other. Neighbors do not know one another except to wave when they drive by. Life is lived at a very fast pace. And while there are some positive aspects to this way of life, what is missing are relationships. There is the need to be with other people in an environment that is conducive to personal growth.

Small group Bible studies are occurring in many congregations with tremendous results. Here the gift of hospitality becomes essential. The willingness to open one's home for these purposes, to provide an atmosphere wherein people can feel so comfortable that they open up and share with each other is essential to the productive success of such groups.

Edna has this gift and her willingness and joy in opening up her home for these kind of purposes is a valuable tool for the congregation she serves. Whether it's a Bible study, a committee meeting or a support gathering, she is one of the first to volunteer to have it in her home. You go into her home and she makes you feel so comfortable that you almost feel as if you are in your own home. This comfortableness enables the work to be accomplished so much better.

Edna believes that in opening her home, she is showing others the kind of love and care God has shown to her. As with so many of the gifts, this gift enables one to see the blessings that come from God. In Edna's case, it is her sense of receiving the love and care of God that motivates her and with this recognition and gratitude comes her need to respond. Edna not only opens her home, but she provides a very loving and caring atmosphere. This is seen through the setting she provides, the joy that radiates when she opens the door to greet people, in the refreshments that are served and in the warmth of her own personality. Altogether, one feels very much at home when visiting in Edna's home.

The gift of hospitality can definitely be used in our setting today. The congregation needs those places to meet away from the church building where warmth and love radiate. When this gift is utilized, it provides a wonderful atmosphere where spiritual growth can occur and relationships, so badly needed, can be developed.

10. Intercession

Intercession is the gift that enables a believer to pray with the certainty that prayer is heard and, when requests are made, answers will come.

Mae caused me to feel so uncomfortable when I first met her. When I was making initial visits to members in the second congregation I served, I spent one afternoon in Mae's home. As we talked about getting started in a new congregation, I mentioned some of my concerns, and immediately she wanted to pray about them. I would mention some possible direction the congregation should go and she would say, "Let's pray about it." While I certainly believed in the power of prayer, I thought she was overdoing it.

As mentioned earlier in this book, this was a point in my life when I did not understand spiritual gifts and, because of this lack of understanding, I did not understand why she was responding as she did. But I learned and in the process was greatly strengthened in my own faith.

Mae had a firm belief that when direction was needed, there was only one place to go: to the Lord in prayer. If answers were needed to serious problems, the only place to go was to the Lord. And without question, answers came! It might not be the answer we wanted, but the right answer would come.

It was this certainty that is most characteristic of this gift. There is no question that Jesus is listening and is responding. There is also no question that He speaks to us, and prayer is the means for listening. Mae could pray for hours. Some of that time she spoke words, but most was spent in listening. She would read devotional material, read passages from the Bible and then, with soft music in the background, she would lean back in her chair and wait for the Lord to speak to her. She was a very unusual lady. But her absolute certainty led others into a meaningful time with prayer.

Mae used her gift in the congregation in several ways. She became a mentor for several members who wanted direction in their prayer lives. She taught a couple of small group courses on spirituality. She developed the first prayer circle which met on a weekly basis. Overall what Mae was able to do through her gift was develop in the congregation the recognition that Jesus was present in our lives, active in our circumstances and wanting to communicate regularly with us.

The gift is a gift of certainty. It is a gift that helps one to understand that prayer is more than just saying a few words and waiting to see what happens. It is communication whereby the one praying is both speaking and listening. The gift helps one to be able to hear and this is accomplished through spiritual study and devotion.

The gift of intercession can also lead to healing. Through prayer, the problems that perplex and overwhelm us are laid before our Lord. The problems can be mental, spiritual or physical. When healing occurs, there is joy and gratitude, but the healing has not occurred because the one with the gift of intercession caused it to happen. It has happened because of the Spirit's action, an action that occurs through prayer. This does not mean that only those with the gift of intercession can pray for healing. What the gift does is to lead people to believe in the power of healing that occurs through prayer.

The gift of intercession opens the door to our Lord. It opens the door to the opportunities for help, the opportunity to give praise and thanks, but above all it gives to the congregation the knowledge that the Lord is working here and now, listening to what we request and responding. One with the gift can give to a congregation such an understanding of prayer that the entire workings of the congregation can be significantly affected.

11. Knowledge

Knowledge is the gift that drives a person to learn, analyze and uncover new insights with regard to the Bible and faith.

In the life story of Martin Luther, it is clear that his greatest joy was the study of Scripture. One can picture him late at night with only a candle for light, searching through the Greek or Hebrew attempting to uncover some new insight that had been heretofore hidden from view. It was this tenacity and drive to discover the truth of Scripture that led him to protest the prevalent views of his time. This tenacity and drive were significant aspects of his gift of knowledge.

Ann has this gift. She is intent upon learning as much about Scripture as possible. She buys all the latest commentaries and has taken courses in Greek and Hebrew from a local seminary. She participates in Bible study groups not only in her own congregation, but in other congregations as well. The pages of her Bible are almost worn out because of her constant use. She has an incredible knowledge of Scripture, but in her mind there is so much more to learn.

As I have observed individuals with this gift, they have this tenacious drive to uncover new truths. They have the belief that there are many truths from the Bible that have yet to be uncovered. In addition, there is much to be learned from truths that have already been discovered.

This gift gives to the gift bearer the capacity to understand, the ability to take in all the facts that are being presented and to select those facts that are consistent with the teachings of Jesus. It is an insatiable desire to learn that drives this gift bearer to use the gift.

But the gift has another element. It is the desire to take what is learned and share it with others. The gift is not for one's own personal use. The gift bearer becomes a conduit through which God's Word becomes known to His children. The gift of knowledge would not be significant unless this element was present. The gift bearer is moved to share with others and this leads to opportunities particularly in a teaching or writing capacity. Some who have the gift of knowledge are very good writers, but very poor teachers, and vice versa. But the gift enables one to find the means to make the truths known.

We have in our universities and seminaries many with the gift of knowledge, and we have been blessed by their gift. But within the congregation there are also believers with this gift. They may not have earned a degree and their learning tools may not be as sophisticated, but they have the desire to learn and to share with others what they have learned. Look in your Bible study groups and inevitably you will find people with this gift. If they do have this gift, often they have not utilized all the avenues to share their knowledge with others. This becomes the role of the church, to take the gift and use whatever means possible to share it with others.

What could be some of these means? The teaching role in the church is most obvious, particularly with the teaching of adults. Another possibility is to have a weekly listening group that, with the pastor, studies the Sunday lessons or a focus group that deals with congregational needs. One with the gift of knowledge could be very helpful in such groups. One I know who possesses this gift leads a weekly Bible study at a local retirement center.

This gift can also be used in writing such as articles for the newsletter or for an Advent or Lenten devotional. Once the gift is discovered, the means to make the gift known become abundant.

12. Leadership

Leadership is the gift that gives a believer the confidence to step forward, give direction and provide motivation to get a task completed or a dream fulfilled.

Simon Peter was a leader from a young age. Everything you read indicates there was little he did where he wasn't the one in charge. He had confidence that he could get the job done and others followed his lead. But he did not possess the gift of leadership until the Pentecost experience.

I point this out because leadership is a trait that one sees in many people. Leaders are confident and able to motivate. They are supremely confident that following their lead will bring about positive results.

But the gift of leadership involves other qualities which only come through the guidance of the Spirit. Take Simon Peter for example. In Jerusalem, he started preaching and no one was paying any attention to him. He was attempting to lead but no one would follow. Then came the entrance of the Holy Spirit. Now Peter possessed the gift of leadership.

The gift of leadership leads a believer to understand who is truly in charge. The Holy Spirit was leading and Peter was simply following that lead. Peter became confident that the Spirit would enable him to do what was right and results would occur. The gift of leadership begins with this understanding, the understanding of who is in charge.

Secondly, the gift enables a gift bearer to lead in directions that are positive for the Church. Many can lead and get others to follow, but the directions may be negative for the Church and for the mission of Christ. The gift bearer is motivated to understand the will of God in a particular situation and then lead others to understand and implement that same will. Therefore the gift is not just one of getting others to follow, but also includes setting the direction in which the group is going to go.

Thirdly, the gift enables one to utilize others in places where they can best serve. The gift bearer recognizes and appreciates the gifts of others. The gift bearer believes that they are together, through God's counsel and call, each to assist in getting the job done.

Finally a person with the gift of leadership exerts that leadership in a positive yet humble manner. With leadership there is frequently the danger of feeling more significant than others, of wanting to be held in high esteem and to receive recognition when the job has been successfully completed. What the gift of leadership does is to enable the gift bearer to see what is happening in a proper perspective. The gift bearer recognizes Who is leading, the assets that have been given through the gifts of others and the nature of the task in fulfilling the mission of Jesus Christ. These are the aspects of the gift that enable the job to be done.

Leadership is one area where many want to serve. We are taught in almost every conceivable way that those who are leaders are those who are the most important, make the most money and achieve the most personal benefits. Therefore many aspire to be leaders. Many can stand before groups and speak, so it is assumed they are leaders. Others can motivate, delegate, and get the job done, so they too are assumed to be leaders.

But the gift of leadership is a gift given to the congregation in order to get its mission fulfilled. One with this gift is motivated toward fulfilling this mission, is positive that the mission can be fulfilled, is able to assist others in using their gifts and can get the direction established. Congregations utilizing this gift move forward and fulfill missions.

Ones with this gift are very effective in leading church boards, long-range task forces and auxiliary groups. Wherever the need exists to enable a purpose to be fulfilled, one with this gift is essential.

13. Mercy

The gift of mercy is the gift that motivates a believer to feel deeply for those in physical, spiritual, or emotional need and then act to meet that need.

In the second chapter of this book, I described an event concerning my friend John and his usage of the gift of mercy. Here I will elaborate on his gift without further describing what occurred in this particular situation. In this event that involved a murder/suicide, John used his gift with the children that were witnesses to what had happened. The gift caused John to immediately feel akin to those in need. He felt the hurt and the pain that had been inflicted. His gift allowed him to know where the pain was and what it was doing to these children. As John told me later, not being able to separate himself from the pain was the most difficult part of the whole experience. But it was his knowing that pain which enabled him to act in the way he did.

Knowing the pain caused him to act in such a way that the pain could be lessened. As John said, "When you feel the pain and you know how badly others are hurting, you have to do something to help them." Therefore what the gift does creates distress on the part of the gift bearer and thereby opens the door to the healing process.

I have a good friend who served a parish in the inner city of a very large metropolitan area. He did a tremendous job of reaching out to people in very difficult circumstances and providing countless ways in which their pain could be lessened. The congregation he served became a model for other congregations, but the programs provided were not the kind of programs normally seen in the inner city. The congregation developed support groups, Bible study groups, healing services and on-site spiritual counseling. From this pastor's perspective, there were needs for food and clothing, employment training, etc., but the greatest pain was mental and spiritual. The end result of their circumstances involved loss of self-esteem and the belief that God didn't love them. So with this pastor's gift of mercy he felt their pain and sought ways to deal with that pain.

Here is a good example of how this gift of mercy was used in the church, but there were also negative factors that need to be explained. This pastor would call me almost every month for spiritual and mental consultation. His gift of feeling the pain was causing him great distress. There is just so much pain anyone can handle, and where his gift was put to use caused his own pain level to be very high. Eventually he had to leave that kind of ministry and serve in another place where the stress level wasn't as high.

I present his story so that you who have the gift and you who will help others discover the gift can recognize how it works as well as the ways in which it can affect the gift bearer. It is such an important gift in the life of a congregation since it brings about so much healing. But the gift bearer must be aware that the gift can also produce a large amount of personal stress. Therefore "leadership" needs to assist gift bearers in not getting burned out or to get away from painful situations every so often in order to relax and recover. Persons with the gift are not always aware of how it can affect them, so those with the gift of leadership must assist.

There are several ways in which the gift bearer can be utilized in the congregation. Normally those possessing this gift are utilized in social ministry areas, serving as volunteers with community agencies or setting up food and clothing shelters within the congregation.

But there are other places where they can be used, such as in visiting congregational members who have suffered a loss or are going through some difficulty. They could be utilized in the development of support groups or therapy groups. Above all, they need to be in direct contact with people who are in painful situations. Their ability to feel and to act prove to be a rich blessing to those they encounter.

14. Music/Vocal

Music/Vocal is the gift that gives a believer the capability and opportunity to present personal witness and inspiration to others through singing.

I was conducting a spiritual gifts workshop in the Midwest and, following my presentations, the group completed an inventory. Once the inventory was completed, they were able to make some determination as to what their gifts might be. One member of the group determined that music/vocal was her gift. Several other members from the group who knew her well came to me and told me that from their experience this was definitely not her gift.

I would imagine that if people were given the chance to choose their spiritual gift, the vast majority would choose this gift. We admire those who have great singing ability and, in our own fantasies, we like to believe that we possess this ability too. But having the ability to sing is not all there is to the gift of music/vocal.

Those who possess the ability of singing and the spiritual gift of singing both have the physical ability, the motivation and the artistic skills necessary to make sounds that bring joy to others. Their talents are usually obvious at an early age and with proper instruction lead them to be enjoyed by many.

But the spiritual gift of music/vocal adds another dimension. It enables one to understand where the gift is coming from and to Whose credit it should be given. It moves the gift bearer to use this gift to God's glory and not to just use it for his or her own personal gain. One with the gift of music/vocal has the abilities, but through the gift has the understanding that leads to how the gift is used.

The gift of music/vocal inspires others to feel the presence and the majesty of God. This gift brings out the emotion of individuals and opens them up to the power of God's love and forgiveness. Perhaps no other means can inspire or move a person as can the usage of this gift.

57

Bonnie has this gift. When she sings, one truly feels the presence of God. Her power and ease in singing moves people to the level of their deepest emotions. In talking with Bonnie, she is humbled by this gift, yet recognizes it as her means of sharing God with others. She is an accomplished artist, but also one whose usage of this gift opens up to others the significance of God in her own life. The gift motivates her to witness to her faith through singing and many have been led to a new understanding of their own faith through her music.

Therefore the gift is one of ability, but above all it is one that brings an understanding. Through this understanding the gift is used in such a way that others are led towards faith or opened up to the presence of the Spirit.

In the congregation, one obvious place where the gift can be used is in the church choir. But there are other places as well. The gift bearer can be used as a soloist during special times such as Christmas and Easter. The gift bearer can be used with the young people as a positive example of how one can witness to his or her faith. Young people are moved by such special skills.

One with the gift of music/vocal is a very powerful addition to any congregation and the use of this gift needs to be extended beyond "normal" channels. It is a gift that brings a special understanding and this understanding can be as powerful a witness as can the use of the gift itself.

15. Music/Instrumental

Music/Instrumental is the gift that gives a believer the desire and capability to express personal faith and provide inspiration and comfort through the playing of a musical instrument.

The gifts of music/vocal and music/instrumental have much in common. They both involve special abilities that are often recognized early in life, and environment, opportunities for training and parental motivation have much to do with musical development. This applies both to those who have the gift and those who don't have the gift. Therefore what is so special about the gift?

From as far back as she can remember, Sheila had this ability and drive to play the piano. With her parents' support and financial capability, she became a very fine pianist. In fact she became so good that she performed with several symphony orchestras. Her abilities led to recording opportunities and she became very well known in the southwest part of the United States.

Her dedication and commitment to the piano left very little time or interest in anything else including participation in the Church. Her parents had no interest here so she was not encouraged in this direction. Furthermore, her time constraints did not allow her time to explore what, if anything, the Church could mean in her life. "From an early age, I had a fascination with the concept of God; but fascination was about as far as it went."

A series of circumstances changed her life. Within a two-year period she lost her mother to cancer and a friend to AIDS. Along with these traumatic experiences, she recognized that something was missing in her life. This led her in the direction of the Church. One day she responded to her growing belief that God was in her life and moving her towards faith. She was baptized. With baptism there came the call to serve God and there came the spiritual gift of music/instrumental.

59

She could already play the instrument and her abilities had carried her to the point of high esteem among her peers and listeners. So what was the gift? As she said, it was a new understanding. Up to this point, she believed that she was the one who had developed her talent to play the piano. It was her ability that enabled her music to be appreciated. Now she realized that it all had come from God and was to be used for His purposes. As with Bonnie in the previous chapter, the gift is the understanding that her abilities are given in order to witness to faith. They are loaned to her by God so that she can bring others to understand the love and presence of God.

I do not believe that the gift is the ability to play the instrument. For instance, someone who is baptized at a later age is not given the spiritual gift of music and suddenly has the ability to perform in a very proficient manner. What the spiritual gift does is to give to one who has abilities the drive, the understanding and the commitment to use that ability to share God's love with the world.

We have all been moved by one who has the talents to play a musical instrument. It brings out the emotions within us and the needs that are present. It is a powerful means to assist each of us in accessing our own commitments. Therefore one who plays this instrument to the glory of God and for the purpose of sharing the faith can reach people in a very significant way.

Within the congregation, persons with the spiritual gift of music/instrumental can impact in powerful ways. They can be utilized as soloists, as leaders in contemporary or traditional worship or in providing significant times of music-based meditations. If you have the gift, use it to the fullest. It is there to reach both the believer and nonbeliever with the power, beauty and majesty of God.

16. Pastor

Pastor is the gift that gives a believer the confidence, capability and compassion to provide spiritual leadership and direction for individuals or groups of individuals.

In the Lutheran Church, Pastor is the term used for one who is ordained. Instead of being called Father, Brother, Reverend or Preacher, one is called Pastor. Therefore when the spiritual gift of pastor is discussed, it is assumed in the Lutheran Church that it refers to one who has gone through specific theological training and is now the leader of a particular congregation. This misunderstanding has created significant problems for both the ordained and those who are members of the congregation.

The gift of pastor is a gift that comes through baptism like all the other gifts. There are members of the clergy who acquired this gift at baptism and are led to be ordained. That, however, is not necessarily the case with everyone. Regardless of who has the gift, ordained or non-ordained, the gift is essential to the life of a congregation.

The gift impacts on the believer in two ways. First is the inner love for Christ that is reflected in the gift bearer's own devotional life. Secondly, the gift bearer is able to recognize that all believers do not move forward in their faith journeys the same way and, therefore, direction is needed. The gift bearer provides the direction, giving to other believers the courage and the motivation to continue on their own faith journeys.

Bob has this gift and is very helpful in assisting others in their journey of faith. Bob has a real sense of God's presence and his own devotional life witnesses to this fact. His devotional life is his source of strength and his days do not begin or end without encountering His Lord through personal devotions. In developing his own devotional life, Bob has discovered a number of scriptural passages and devotional books

61

that have proven very helpful. These devotional aids are then shared with others who are wanting spiritual direction. What Bob's gift does is to motivate him to share with others what he has discovered for himself. His own faith journey becomes a guide to help others on their faith journeys.

In a congregation, those believers who have this gift can be utilized in a number of ways. The gift bearer can serve as a spiritual director working with individuals or small groups interested in developing their own spiritual lives. What the gift bearer does is help others see the importance of having a spiritual foundation and to develop it through persistence and determination. For many believers this is difficult. Therefore, one with this gift provides a real source of strength not only for the individual believer but for the congregation as well.

17. Service

The gift of service is the gift that enables a believer to work gladly behind the scenes in order that God's work is fulfilled.

Roger was always there when you needed him. In one congregation I served, the buildings we used were multi-purpose. This meant there was a constant need to move tables, slide partitions and set up chairs. It was not the most popular job in the congregation, but I always knew Roger would come to help. You didn't even need to call him, he would just appear. When a special program was presented, he would be the first to arrive, making sure everything was in place; and he was the last to leave, making sure all was in readiness for the next event. He was not the paid custodian, but you would not have known it from all the work he did.

One day I expressed my appreciation for his help, and he seemed genuinely embarrassed by what I said. "I can't do what so many of the other members can do like teach and sing, so this is about the only way I can serve. I am very glad I can help in this way."

Without Roger, our congregation would not have been able to operate as smoothly. His humble service allowed many programs to be carried out and the buildings to be in constant use. He was an example to all of us of what ministry was about. He expected nothing from those utilizing his service; he was only too glad to help.

Once we had a special night in his honor. No one in the congregation was loved or appreciated more than Roger. But we had to make it a surprise or else he probably would not have come. He was embarrassed by all that was said. When the president of the congregation mentioned that through the years no one had meant more to the congregation than he, Roger burst into tears. What a witness to humble service.

The gift of service gives to the gift bearer that humbleness so lacking in today's society. The willingness to put self second and the good of the mission first is all too rare. Therefore we need examples such as Roger.

In all congregations, there are members present with this gift. It is a gift to be noticed and appreciated. It is not so vital that the gift bearer is aware of this gift as it is for the congregation. The gift bearer witnesses to the servanthood of Christ and to the power of servanthood in our own day.

18. Teaching

*Teaching is the gift that enables a believer to com-
municate a personal understanding of the Bible and faith
in such a way that it becomes clear and understood by
others.*

I was twelve years old when my father took me to hear Dr.
Paul Tillich, the world-famous theologian, speak at Vander-
bilt University in Nashville, Tennessee. He was giving a series
of lectures for the school of religion, and one of these lectures
was open to the public. We sat there for about one hour as
Dr. Tillich spoke to a very large group of people. When the
speech was over, we were walking to the car when my father
said, "That was the most brilliant speech I have ever heard.
I don't have the faintest idea what he said, but it was the most
brilliant speech I have ever heard."

I am not saying that Dr. Tillich did not have the gift of
teaching, but at least for my father, the gift wasn't in evidence.
We have all heard public speakers who were obviously brilliant and filled with knowledge of the subject matter, yet un-
able to communicate in a way that is understandable.

Dr. Williard Allbeck did not have this problem. He taught
church history when I was in seminary. He could take the most
difficult event from history and present it in such a way that
you felt as if you were there and witnessing the scene being
described. He made history easy. While we were well aware
of his own knowledge, what struck us in his classes was his
way of making all that happened sound so easy to understand.
He could explain events and why they happened; historical
characters came alive and their motivations for actions became
obvious. You would understand and appreciate what had
happened.

He could also make you keenly aware of God's movement
within the event itself or within the life of the individual he
was discussing. Nothing ever occurred historically without the

movement of God. His belief system was clear as he presented the years of history to his students.

The spiritual gift of teaching gives to the believer the thirst for knowledge, a passion to learn. The believer is moved to know as much as possible and to always be in the learning mode. But the passion for learning isn't for the believer's own sake; it is to be shared with others.

This gift allows the gift bearer to share the content of his or her teaching in such a way that others comprehend what is being taught. The gift bearer sees clearly an idea/thought and then translates it in such a way that the students wonder why they had never known it before. The greatest compliment that one with the spiritual gift of teaching can receive is that he or she made it so easy to understand.

It is not hard to imagine where a gift bearer with this gift can be used in the parish. Wherever believers gather to learn is where the gift bearer desires to be. Whether it's in the classroom, small-group study or the pulpit, one with the gift of teaching can be a real blessing in the congregation.

But one word of caution. This gift is not at home in administering a church school or running an education program. The gift is to be used in teaching others and this is the reason our Lord has called teachers to the congregation.

19. Wisdom

Wisdom is the gift that allows the believer to sort through opinions, facts and thoughts in order to determine what solution would be best for the individual believer or the community of believers.

Whenever one thinks of wisdom in spiritual terms, thoughts often turn toward the story of Solomon in the Old Testament. Out of all the gifts Solomon could possess, he chose wisdom. Then in the story of the two women each claiming to be the mother of a child, we see this gift put to use. Solomon sorts out all the facts, lays out a suggestion and then from the responses decides what is right.

Wisdom is a gift that gives to the gift bearer the ability to see beyond mere words and ideas, to see beyond the facade that is often put in place and to sort out all the facts, so that in the long run truth prevails. It is a gift that allows the believer to get to the bottom line, cut through all that gets in the way of truth and make a determination that is in the best interest of all concerned.

The gift of wisdom gives the gift bearer a mind like that of a computer. The mind takes in, sorts through, sifts out and comes to a conclusion. Therefore one with the gift can listen to a number of views being expressed with regard to a particular situation or project, sort through what is being discussed and determine what is the best direction for the individual or group to take.

There are some similarities between the gift of discernment and the gift of wisdom. Both involve sorting through the information presented, both involve determining what might be God's will, and both involve giving direction. The difference is that the gift of discernment gives to the gift bearer the ability to see what is right and wrong, what is good and evil, what is in accord with God's will for His people and what is in accord with Satan's will. The gift of wisdom is much more oriented toward direction. The gift bearer can see the end result of possible directions we can take. All the directions being discussed may have merit and be good directions, but only one will really work, and that is where the gift of wisdom becomes so helpful.

For instance, a building project is planned by a congregation. The gift of discernment can be very useful in determining if the motivation and intent of the project is good or evil, for our human frailty can make even the noblest of tasks an evil doing. The gift of wisdom helps determine the direction that needs to be taken in order to complete the task. One with the gift of wisdom can sit and listen to many ideas and suggestions and, through this gift, can sort through all that has been said and decide what direction will work.

The gift of wisdom can be utilized in many ways within the congregation. One with this gift is very helpful whenever long-range task forces gather together, when special project committees are formed and can be very useful on the church board. The gift bearer can also provide significant counsel to those who are making life decisions such as in their business dealings or with regard to family relationships. The usage of this gift can be vital to the ability of a congregation to most effectively and efficiently fulfill its mission.

20. Writing

Writing is the gift that gives a believer the ability to translate Biblical truth into a written form that can edify, instruct and strengthen the community of believers.

Gene has the spiritual gift of writing. Not a day goes by that he isn't writing about something that he is thinking about or has seen. His word processor is his communication tool with the world and with himself. Even if his words are not published, the process of writing opens a door to him for understanding and inspiration. "As I am writing, words come together in ways that give meaning and understanding to what I'm thinking about. I write the words; but once written, they are like a message that is given back to me. I am often surprised by what I read even though I am the one that has put those words on paper. It may sound weird, but as I read what I have put on paper, it is as if God is talking with me and sharing some direction or word of inspiration."

As with music/vocal, music/instrumental and craftsmanship, writing is an art form. It gives to the gift bearer a mental picture or a thought or the outline of a story that can be put into a written form. Words flow as the image is being put onto paper. The gift gives clarity and order along with understanding and inspiration.

The gift opens the door for others to know and understand the will and purposes of God. The writer is utilized by God so that others are reached and moved to spiritual understandings. Through the words produced God is sharing a message with others. It is a very spiritual experience for the writer and he or she feels a responsibility and an urgency to get this message to others. This is not to suggest that, through this gift, God takes a person by the hand and produces a message. One's own experiences and viewpoints shape what is written, but the gift bearer is led by the gift to understand that the Spirit's counsel and guidance is involved in what is produced.

One with the gift of writing can be utilized in many ways within the congregation. The first thought is a column in the newsletter, but there are other means that can be used. One with the gift can produce an Advent or Lenten devotional. The gift bearer might write a drama or a song that can be used by the choir. The gift does not give to the writer the ability to write anything; the kind of writing is based on the individual skills. But once that is determined, the usage can prove extremely valuable.

Chapter 4

Implementation

A plan of implementation is needed in order to make spiritual gifts a focus of the congregation. It is needed for several reasons. First, there are probably not many congregational members who know anything about the subject. Particularly is this true for congregational members whose denomination origin is Europe. Secondly, the theological position that at baptism one is called and a gift is given is a position foreign to many of the baptized. Therefore steps must be taken in order to introduce this subject to the congregation.

The group that must first be introduced to spiritual gifts are those elected by the congregation to govern the overall program. As with all new ideas, little if anything will be successful in the congregation without the support and encouragement of this group. If leaders, through study, come to believe that the use of gifts is vital for the congregation, then the possibility for implementation is greatly enhanced.

Many council, vestry or session meetings begin with a devotional period. You could, for example, use the chapters of this book as an outline for these devotionals over a period of several months. Start with the theological basis for gifts. It is imperative that the study begin here, for unless the members are convinced that a power is present that is not being used, the study will get nowhere.

In discussing the theological basis for spiritual gifts, consider the calls of Moses, Jeremiah, Simon Peter and Saint Paul. Review each of these calls, their circumstances and the powers given to each one in order to complete their calls. Take your time; go only as fast as the group can handle. Everyone needs to understand theologically where these gifts have been used in order to understand how the gifts can be used today.

Following the theological discussion, proceed to a study of the gifts themselves. In this book, you have a narrative on each gift along with a definition and scriptural basis. Start with the scriptural references, then read the definition and then the narrative. The goal is that each member will recognize what gift is theirs.

Following the study, proceed to the inventory. Once it is completed, people should study the gift they believe is theirs and the ways it can be implemented in the congregation.

Once this study has been completed, a process has been developed that can be useful with other groups in the congregation. Here the key leaders may decide to implement a particular plan of action. Here is a way of implementation that has been successful in many congregations.

A three-part sermon series is the first step. In the sermon series, focus first on the calls that we have recognized from the Bible. Second, focus on the call that comes through baptism and the gift that is given. Third, relay the call of the congregation and how the call is fulfilled through the usage of the spiritual gifts.

You have now placed the idea of spiritual gifts before the congregation. There are some who have more understanding than others but interest has been generated. The next step is to meet with groups.

It is assumed that the pastor has been the primary teacher up to this point. But now with the introduction to groups, it would be helpful to have others lead as well. Perhaps the president of the congregation would lead a series or someone else who has the gift of teaching. With two or more teachers, the possibility of reaching a larger number of members is increased. It is important that as many members as possible be introduced as quickly as possible because of the interest that has been generated.

Congregations who have used this process have found women's circles, men's groups, Bible study groups, Sunday morning adult forums are all possibilities. Some congregations have a one-day seminar and bring together officers and program committee members from all the groups in the congregation. The key is that more members in strategic positions within the congregation are becoming involved.

One group that every congregation should not overlook in the plan of action is the youth. Young people are always interested in knowing about themselves, and this study impacts into a strategic area of their lives. In the congregation I am serving, I make this a part of the confirmation curriculum. Confirmation is the two-year program for seventh and eighth grade young people where the doctrines and beliefs of the church are taught. I have a three-week series on spiritual gifts and then, during the fourth week, they take the inventory. I am not sure they are old enough and have experienced enough to make a correct determination as to their gift, but it introduces them to the fact that our Lord has called them to serve Him and has given to each one a gift to enable His work to be done. I have not led a group of confirmation students through this study where the interest wasn't extremely high.

In addition to confirmation, this series could be presented in a youth retreat, in the high school class or in regular youth group meetings. I have found that this study is not very meaningful if the young people are below the seventh grade. But for those who are older it is a wonderful way of introducing God's call in a way that is specific and meaningful.

Another group that should be included in the plan of action are new members. When members join the congregation, interest is high, so this is a perfect time to introduce this process. I have a five-session course for new members beginning with the Sunday they join and continuing for four additional weeks. The spiritual gift study is carried out during the last three sessions. In the final session, they take the inventory and are assisted in determining where they might serve in the congregation. It has been exciting to see the results of this study and the immediate impact so many new members have on the congregation.

By focusing on the governing body, the congregation in worship, the leadership, young people and new members, it will not be long before many congregational members have completed the process. Now comes a very significant step. The results of all the inventories must be compiled so that you know what gifts are present in what members. When responsibilities develop in the congregation, this compilation should be used in determining who can serve in what capacity.

One final note concerning implementation. It must be done within a relatively short period of time. As the saying goes, "Strike while the iron is hot." The size of the congregation will have a direct bearing on the length of time it takes to implement the program, but it should not take more than one year to implement the initial plan. Once the plan is implemented, then the leadership group needs to insure that it is continued with new members and new leadership who have not yet completed the study.

Not every member of the congregation will participate in the process. This is a given and must be recognized. Fringe members will often not participate for two reasons. One, the church is simply not a priority except when they are in need of baptism, confirmation, marriage or burial. Second, others want to receive from the congregation rather than give.

This second reason is also true for some active members. Religion, from their viewpoint, is between themselves and God. The idea of spiritual gifts does not enter into that line of thinking. They enter into congregational life from the perspective of receiving spiritual benefits and the notion that there is a call involved or a spiritual direction involving the usage of their talents is too much for them to handle. Some may be so locked into the way congregational life has always been conducted in the past that they are closed to anything new or different. I have found others closed to the idea simply out of fear. They are afraid of something different as it might open the door to something else that is different and this fear closes them to any possibility for change.

Even though not everyone will get on board, if the elected leaders actually lead here and the process is continued as suggested, spiritual gifts will become a vital part of your congregational life and you will be amazed at all that happens.

Chapter 5

Definition And Scriptural Reference

In this chapter you will find a list of the gifts, their definitions and scriptural references. The scriptural references will either be references where the gifts are listed or references how the gifts have been used. I have also included a space for personal comments. This is your space where you can jot down notes or write the name of someone you know who might possess the gift. As you read through the definitions and references, take the time to quietly and prayerfully reflect on what you think your gift might be. In the next chapter, you will have the opportunity to complete an inventory and see if your first thought on your own gift was correct.

1. Administration
Administration is the gift that enables a believer to formulate, direct, and carry out plans necessary to fulfill a purpose.
1 Corinthians 12:28
Acts 14:23
Comment:

2. Apostle

Apostle is the gift that gives a believer the courage and the urgency to express faith in settings where the Gospel is rarely heard.

1 Corinthians 12:28
Acts 20:17-21
Romans 1:14-16
    Comment:

3. Craftsmanship/Artistry

Craftsmanship/Artistry is the gift that gives the believer the skill of creating artistic expressions that produce a spiritual response of strength and inspiration.

Exodus 31:1-11
Psalm 149:3a
    Comment:

4. Discernment

Discernment is the gift that motivates a believer to seek God's will and purpose and apply that understanding to individual and congregational situations.

John 16:6-15
Romans 9:1
1 Corinthians 2:9-16
    Comment:

5. Evangelism

Evangelism is the gift that moves believers to reach non-believers in such a way that they are baptized and become active forces in the Christian community.

Matthew 28:16-20
Ephesians 4:11-17
Acts 2:36-40
Comment:

6. Exhortation

Exhortation is a gift that moves the believer to reach out with Christian love and presence to people in personal conflict or facing a spiritual void.

John 14:1
2 Timothy 1:16-18
3 John 5-8
Comment:

7. Faith

Faith is the gift that gives a believer the eyes to see the Spirit at work and the ability to trust the Spirit's leading with no sense where it all might lead.

Genesis 12:1-4a
Mark 5:25-34
1 Thessalonians 1:8-10
Comment:

8. Giving

Giving is the gift that enables a believer to recognize God's blessings and to respond to those blessings by generously and sacrificially giving of one's material resources.

Luke 21:1-4

2 Corinthians 9:6-15

Romans 12:13a

Comment:

9. Hospitality

Hospitality is the gift that causes a believer to joyfully open his or her home for meetings and overnight visitors.

Luke 10:38

Romans 16:23a

Romans 12:13b

Comment:

10. Intercession

Intercession is the gift that enables a believer to pray with the certainty that prayer is heard and, when requests are made, answers will come.

Matthew 6:6-15

Luke 22:42

Ephesians 6:18

Comment:

11. Knowledge

Knowledge is the gift that drives a person to learn, analyze and uncover new insights with regard to the Bible and faith.

1 Corinthians 12:8
Romans 12:2
1 Corinthians 14:6
Comment:

12. Leadership

Leadership is the gift that gives a believer the confidence to step forward, give direction and provide motivation to get a task completed or a dream fulfilled.

Romans 12:8
John 21:15-17
Comment:

13. Mercy

The gift of mercy is the gift that motivates a believer to feel deeply for those in physical, spiritual or emotional need and then act to meet that need.

Luke 7:12-15
Matthew 25:34-36
Luke 10:30-37
Comment:

14. Music/Vocal

Music/Vocal is the gift that gives a believer the capability and opportunity to present personal witness and inspiration to others through singing.

Psalm 96:1-9
Psalm 100:1-2
Psalm 149:1-2
Comment:

15. Music/Instrumental

Music/Instrumental is the gift that gives a believer the desire and capability to express personal faith and provide inspiration and comfort through the playing of a musical instrument.

Psalm 33:1-3
Psalm 150
1 Samuel 16:14-23
Comment:

16. Pastor

Pastor is the gift that gives a believer the confidence, capability and compassion to provide spiritual leadership and direction for individuals or groups of individuals.

1 Timothy 4:12-16
1 Timothy 3:1-13
2 Timothy 4:1-2
Comment:

17. Service

The gift of service is the gift that enables a believer to work gladly behind the scenes in order that God's work is fulfilled.

Luke 23:50-54

Romans 16:1-16

Philippians 2:19-23

Comment:

18. Teaching

Teaching is the gift that enables a believer to communicate a personal understanding of the Bible and faith in such a way that it becomes clear and understood by others.

Acts 18:24-28

Matthew 5:1-12

1 Corinthians 12:28

Comment:

19. Wisdom

Wisdom is the gift that allows the believer to sort through opinions, facts, and thoughts in order to determine what solution would be best for the individual believer or the community of believers.

James 3:13-18

1 Corinthians 2:6-13

2 Chronicles 1:7-11

Comment:

20. Writing

Writing is the gift that gives a believer the ability to translate Bible truth into a written form that can edify, instruct and strengthen the community of believers.

1 John 2:1-6, 12-14
1 Timothy 3:14-15
John 26:30-31
    Comment:

Chapter 6

The Inventory

In order to complete the inventory, note that beside each number, there are three statements. Read each statement and then rate it as to how well the statement describes your own life experiences. The scale you will use is 0-2. Place a 0 beside the statement if it has no application to your own experience. Put a 1 if you have found, on occasion, that it applies to you. Put a 2 if you believe the statement clearly describes your own experience. Be honest with yourself but recognize that no statement applies all the time. Our tendency is to be either too honest or too humble and that will not be of benefit in this effort. Once you have rated all three statements, total your score and move on to the next set of statements.

1. Statements
_____a. When presented a goal or objective, I immediately think of steps that need to be taken in order to achieve the desired result.
_____b. I feel excited when I am organizing thoughts, ideas, hopes or dreams into a specific plan.
_____c. In organizing, directing and motivating people to achieve a purpose, I have been pleased to see the result.
Total for all three statements_____

2. Statements

____a. I am compelled to express my faith despite the possibility of personal consequences.

____b. When speaking with a nonbeliever or a group of nonbelievers, I am not afraid to give witness to my faith.

____c. While some consider my witnessing to be offensive, others have been led through it to recognize the Lordship of Jesus Christ.

Total for all three statements____

3. Statements

____a. I express my faith through artistic means.

____b. I can translate into artistic form what I first see in my imagination.

____c. I have been told that my artistic work gives spiritual strength to believers and nonbelievers.

Total for all three statements____

4. Statements

____a. My faith demands that I seek out God's will and purpose.

____b. I have assisted individuals in assessing whether their personal decisions are good or evil in the eyes of God.

____c. In the congregation I am often asked if a particular direction being discussed is motivated by the desire to fulfill God's will or by selfish human interests.

Total for all three statements____

5. Statements

____a. I am seized with the desire to lead nonbelievers to be baptized.

____b. I seek out nonbelievers in order to open them to accepting the Lordship of Jesus Christ for themselves.

____c. I do not find it difficult to share what Jesus means to me with nonbelievers.

Total for all three statements____

6. Statements

_____a. I am moved by those who through conflict or sorrow are wavering in faith.

_____b. When I know someone is facing a crisis, I go to provide support and care.

_____c. Those who are questioning their faith come to me for help.

Total for all three statements_____

7. Statements

_____a. I am certain of the Spirit's presence in my life and the lives of others.

_____b. My trust in the Spirit's presence when I encounter times of personal crisis is a source of strength for others.

_____c. I can see great things happening or about to happen in my congregation and I am not deterred by the pessimism or caution of others.

Total for all three statements_____

8. Statements

_____a. I am blessed by my Lord each day and gladly respond to these blessings by giving liberally.

_____b. I manage my money in such a way that I can gladly give much of it to the work of the church.

_____c. When I receive money unexpectedly, one of my first thoughts is to share this gift through the church.

Total for all three statements_____

9. Statements

_____a. I get excited and feel blessed when visitors come and share my home.

_____b. I am frequently asked to open my home for small group Bible studies or cottage meetings.

_____c. "You made me feel at home" are words often expressed when visitors leave my home.

Total for all three statements_____

10. Statements

____a. I know that through my daily prayers, God hears and responds to me.

____b. I become so absorbed in my prayer life that the doorbell or phone can ring, and I don't hear it.

____c. Believers have asked me to pray for healing in their lives, and through my prayers God has evidenced healing in them.

Total for all three statements____

11. Statements

____a. I am driven to learn as much as I can about the Bible and faith.

____b. Not one day would be complete without time for Bible study and thought.

____c. My studies have proven helpful to others on their journeys of faith.

Total for all three statements____

12. Statements

____a. I am a take-charge person and possess the confidence that when others follow my direction, the goal or task will be completed.

____b. When I am in a group, I will often be placed in charge.

____c. People have said they like to work with me because I am so convinced that together a task will be successfully completed.

Total for all three statements____

13. Statements

____a. When I see a person in need, I am moved to meet that need.

____b. I feel an urgency to provide housing for the homeless, food for the starving, comfort for those in distress.

____c. People have been surprised by how at ease I am working with those who are suffering in mind, body or spirit.

Total for all three statements____

14. Statements

____a. I love to express my faith by singing.

____b. I have sung before groups and felt a real sense of God's presence.

____c. I am grateful and humbled that my singing has provided inspiration and hope for others on their faith journeys.

Total for all three statements____

15. Statements

____a. I love to express my faith through a musical instrument.

____b. By playing a musical instrument, inspiration has been provided for both myself and others.

____c. Others have been moved by my playing to such an extent that they have shared these experiences with me.

Total for all three statements____

16. Statements

____a. I am motivated to provide spiritual leadership for those on their faith journeys.

____b. I have responsibility for providing spiritual guidance to an individual believer or group of believers.

____c. People have come to me for spiritual help and it has developed into a long-term relationship.

Total for all three statements____

17. Statements

____a. I am needed to work behind the scenes to enable ministries of the church to be successful.

____b. Leaders of the congregation tell me that without my willingness to do the unnoticed jobs, their work would be more difficult.

____c. When I turn the lights out or take down the tables, work in the kitchen or put the chairs away I feel good that I have served my Lord.

Total for all three statements____

18. Statements

_____a. My greatest joy is to communicate Bible truth in such a way that it becomes real and understood by others.

_____b. I want to express my faith by assisting others to discover the truths contained in the Bible and church doctrine.

_____c. Students have told me that I can take the most difficult idea, thought or fact and make it understandable.

Total for all three statements_____

19. Statements

_____a. When a challenge is presented, I usually can determine a solution.

_____b. People come to me for help in applying Christian faith and values to personal solutions.

_____c. When direction is needed in the congregation, I am generally asked for my view.

Total for all three statements_____

20. Statements

_____a. I am able to take a thought or idea and put it into a clear and inspiring form.

_____b. If I am not writing, I don't feel complete or satisfied.

_____c. My writings have been helpful to others in understanding Bible truth.

Total for all three statements_____

Once you have completed the inventory, find the two sets of statements for which you have given yourself the most total points. On the lines below put the numbers of the two highest sets of statements along with the total points for each set of statements. For example, if set of statements #20 has the highest total put it on the line below and beside it place the total points. Do the same for your next highest total.

Set of statements number_____   Total Points_____

Set of statements number_____   Total Points_____

Now go back to the preceding chapter and find the gift that corresponds to your highest set of statements number. Next, find the gift that corresponds to your second highest set of statements number. For instance if #1 is your highest set of statements, that would be the gift of administration; if your high number is #15, that would be the gift of music/instrumental. Once you have identified the gifts, write them in the assigned spaces below. Place the gift with the highest total in the number one position and the gift with the second highest total in the number two position.

Number 1 gift_____

Number 2 gift_____

If you are surprised by what has resulted, there are two ways that you can test the accuracy. First, check with some people who know you well and ask them if they agree or disagree with the determination. A gift can be verifiable. Secondly, you can try the gift out in ways suggested in chapter three and see if you find the work exciting, fulfilling and successful. If the gift is yours, all three results will be apparent.

Let's look at your point totals. If your high point total is in the 5-6 range, there is a strong possibility this gift is yours and you have already identified and used it. If your high number is in the 2-4 range, use the gift and see how it works for you. It could be that you are being modest in your ratings or the gift has not yet surfaced completely at this point in your life. If you do try it out, you will find very quickly if there is evidence to believe that it is your gift.

If your highest rating is below 2, then you need to give a closer look to the statements. Perhaps someone you know well could work through the inventory with you. *You do have one of the gifts listed.* For some it takes longer than others to determine, but one of these gifts is yours. Don't get down on yourself or feel less faithful than others. Just keep working at it — the understanding will come.

Once all the work has been done to determine your gift, read through the narrative in chapter three. See how your experience coincides with others who have the same gift. Then, above all, start using the gift in the congregation if you aren't already doing so. Your pastor could be very helpful in this process.

There is a possibility that you could have two or even three gifts with the same high totals. If that is the case, you might have a gift mix; in other words, you might possess multiple gifts. A gift mix could be very helpful in a number of ways. For example, the gifts of administration and leadership give to the gifts bearer the opportunity of being not only one who can lead, but also one who understands clearly the steps that must be taken to reach the goal. The gift mix of teaching and writing can result in a gifts bearer having two outlets for his or her witnessing. The gift mix of music/vocal and knowledge opens the door for one not only to provide inspiration but also understanding. There are all kinds of possibilities that a gift mix can create, and it is up to you and those who work with you to take advantage of them and utilize them for our Lord's purpose.

You have gone through an exciting process. Pray about the results that have come, give thanks for the gift(s) that have been given and seek His guidance in your next step of faith.

Conclusion

Through this book, I hope that you have discovered your own spiritual gift and have become excited about the possibilities spiritual gifts can bring to a congregation. Certainly congregations can exist and fulfill mission without a thorough understanding of spiritual gifts, but through the understanding there is so much more that can be done.

What the understanding and usage of spiritual gifts can do is twofold. First, it accentuates the view that ministry in a congregation is a shared responsibility. Every member is called into the congregation to serve in some specific way. Secondly, it helps a congregation to focus on placing each member where his or her gift can best be used. So often, members do not know where they can serve and the understanding of these gifts can help meet this need.

The understanding and usage of these gifts has been especially helpful for me as an ordained minister. For years I held the view that I was the only one called into a congregation to minister. The responsibility of the congregation to fulfill the mission was solely mine. It was an incredible responsibility that was virtually impossible to fulfill. I was also aware that I did not have all the gifts necessary for the congregation to function most effectively. I am not gifted in those areas that assist the baptized in spiritual direction and crisis intervention. I would try to assist, but it was very difficult for me to accomplish. Upon learning about these gifts, I now utilize those in the congregation who have these gifts and the ministry is much more effectively carried out and individual needs are better handled. No longer do I believe that I have to be everything to everyone and that has given me a new understanding of my calling.

Spiritual gifts open doors. They open the door for each baptized member to understand more fully the special place God has for service. They open the door for the baptized to understand the team effort that is needed in order for missions to be accomplished. Above all, they open the door for a focusing on mission, the purpose that brings congregational members together.

Finally, you will notice in this book that certain spiritual gifts listed by Saint Paul are not included. You will also notice that some gifts I have listed are not specifically mentioned by the same apostle. I have focused on those gifts that can best be implemented in parish life. I have also included some gifts listed by Saint Paul under other gift titles.

I have not included speaking in tongues for two reasons. First, there is much misunderstanding about this gift. Even Saint Paul was rather appalled by its usage. Secondly, Martin Luther saw the gift of speaking in tongues as valuable in one's own devotional life but not valuable in the practice of the congregation. So it has been omitted.

Prophecy is not listed specifically, though I believe this gift is included in the gifts "knowledge" and "discernment." Both these gifts include the ability to understand God's will and purpose and, therefore, can assist the congregation and individual Christian to better determine present and future actions. The use of prophecy in the Bible is always on the basis of the present situation and what will happen if circumstances and actions do not change.

Finally, I have not included healing in my listing of gifts. I include it in the gift of intercession. Healing does not occur through one's own actions, but through the prayers that are offered. The gift bearer may lay hands on an individual but then it is through prayer that the healing by God can occur.

May God richly bless you in your own spiritual gift understanding and may this understanding lead to new opportunities for mission throughout the Church.

Pastor Neal Boese has served congregations in Texas, Nebraska and is presently the Senior Pastor of Gloria Dei Lutheran Church in Crestview Hills, Kentucky.

In 1982, he was selected as a Pastor/Evangelist for the Lutheran Church in America and in 1985 he became the Director of Evangelism for the Michigan Synod-Lutheran Church in America. In 1994, he was named a Partner in Mission for the Evangelical Lutheran Church In America.

Pastor Boese has written two previous books. They are *Why Can't We Grow? We Can!* and *Seven Steps And You Will Grow*. He has also written numerous articles for denominational magazines. He co-authored a spiritual gifts inventory for the Evangelical Lutheran Church In America in 1995.

In addition to parish duties and writing, Pastor Boese conducts outreach and spiritual gift workshops throughout the United States.

Order Form

Additional copies may be ordered for church council members, Bible study groups, evangelism task forces and leaders in evangelism and education. Please complete this order form and send to:

Seven Steps Ministries   Fairway Press
P.O. Box 18036   Or   517 S. Main Street
Erlanger, Kentucky 41018   P.O. Box 4503
                                Lima, Ohio 45802-4503

I want _____ copies of SPIRITUAL GIFTS. Enclosed is my check for _____ which includes postage and handling charges. Our tax exempt number is _____.

copies 1-10 $6.95 each
copies 11-25 $6.25 each
copies 26-50 $5.50 each
copies 51 + $5.00 each

Postage & Handling Charges
Up to $25.00 $2.00
$25.00 to $50.00 $3.50
$50.00 to $100.00 $5.00
Over $100.00   Billed Directly

SEND BOOKS TO:

_____

_____

_____

**Make Checks Payable To: Seven Steps Ministries
Or: Fairway Press**